Life
BRIGHTENERS
(for)
Couples

H. Curtis & Karen McDaniel

WATERBROOK
PRESS

LIFE BRIGHTENERS FOR COUPLES
PUBLISHED BY WATERBROOK PRESS
2375 Telstar Drive, Suite 160
Colorado Springs, Colorado 80920
A division of Random House, Inc.

ISBN 1-57856-732-7

Printed in Canada
2004—First Edition

10 9 8 7 6 5 4 3 2 1

This book is designed to help spouses encourage one another and to keep in touch when one or both are away from home. More than twenty-two years ago, God introduced us to each other through a grief process. Both of us were mourning the deaths of our fathers; yet while we were in a Sunday school class studying Scripture, God provided an opportunity for us to meet, and our relationship blossomed. From those tough times to the present, we continue to learn that, for contentment in marriage, an ounce of encouragement is worth a pound of well-being. So, in light of God's encouragement to us, we dedicate this book back to him, who is the Author and Creator of this beautiful institution called marriage. May he use his Word to strengthen and enrich other marriages, and may he alone receive the glory.

One last word: encourage others to go to Sunday school. You never know, God may introduce them to their spouse!

ACKNOWLEDGMENTS

Special thanks go to the following:

To our friends Jeff and Kelli Hill for reading the manuscript and offering great suggestions in the topic section.

To our many family members, friends, and faithful prayer partners in Virginia; the St. Louis area; Montgomery, Alabama; Middle Tennessee; southern Kentucky; Fort Lauderdale, Florida; and Butler, Pennsylvania, for their faithful intercession for this work.

Thanks to all of you for your help, encouragement, and prayers for us.

Keep in Touch When You're Out of Arm's Reach

There's something contagious about encouragement. We all need it in our daily lives. But sometimes the people who are closest to us have the greatest difficulty knowing how to light up our lives.

It's not that spouses don't want to encourage each other. Most would like to send their mate a daily word of inspiration. They'd love to pass along a verse of Scripture that addresses an issue that's affecting their work or marriage. In addition, they'd like to give their spouse an inspiring thought to encourage him or her in the midst of job or family tensions. But often they don't have the time, or they become frustrated searching for just the right verse.

Now you can use *Life Brighteners for Couples* to regularly send a note that will touch your spouse's heart. Each of the ninety Life Brighteners features a timely verse of Scripture with related thoughts designed to help you encourage and build up your spouse.

How to Use Life Brighteners

Each day, or as often as you want, you can tear out a perforated page and place a Life Brightener note in your spouse's briefcase, portfolio, purse, or workout bag. If your spouse travels regularly, put one or a few in his or her luggage.

The Life Brighteners are organized under thirty life issues that all couples face, with three pertinent messages under each topic. The back of each page gives you an opportunity to write a prayer or a personal note of love and encouragement for the day. With the perforated pages, this system will take mere seconds, but the impact will last all day long!

Each day's Life Brightener enables you to:

- Encourage your spouse with a biblical pick-me-up for the day.
- Communicate love and thoughtfulness while you're apart.
- Equip your spouse with truths that he or she can use in being a witness for Christ.
- Supply timely scripture and related thoughts that address issues your spouse is facing at the moment.

As you use these Life Brighteners, ask the Holy Spirit to minister to your spouse's heart.

I pray that out of his glorious riches
he may strengthen you with power through his Spirit
in your inner being, so that Christ may dwell
in your hearts through faith.

EPHESIANS 3:16-17

You're in My Heart

It is right for me to feel this way...

since I have you in my heart....

PHILIPPIANS 1:7

Today's Life Brightener

You're not only on God's mind today, but you're also in my heart. Know that today and every day I love you deeply.

Special Notes:

●--●

●--●

●--●

●--●

My Heart's Longing

God can testify how I long for all of you
with the affection of Christ Jesus.

PHILIPPIANS 1:8

Today's Life Brightener

I long to see your smile and feel your touch. You're a tremendous blessing to me—one of God's very best gifts.

Special Notes:

The Joy of My Life

...you whom I love and long for,

my joy and crown...

PHILIPPIANS 4:1

Today's Life Brightener

God gave me such deep happiness and contentment when he brought us together. Thanks for being the person you are!

Special Notes:

●--●

●--●

●--●

●--●

APPRECIATION

I'm Thankful for You

I thank my God every time I remember you.

PHILIPPIANS 1:3

Today's Life Brightener

God brought you to mind, and I realized how thankful I am for you. I'm praying for you today because you are so valuable to me!

Special Notes:

Faith That Grows

…your faith is growing more and more….

2 THESSALONIANS 1:3

Today's Life Brightener

When I see your trust in God, it does something for me. Your faith strengthens my own faith!

Special Notes:

I Appreciate Your Love

...ever since I heard about your...love for all the saints,
I have not stopped giving thanks for you....

EPHESIANS 1:15-16

Today's Life Brightener

Today I thanked God for you because of your love for me. You motivate me to have a grateful heart.

Special Notes:

The Attitude of Christ

Your attitude should be the same as that of Christ Jesus.

PHILIPPIANS 2:5

Today's Life Brightener

When we have the attitude of Christ, God gives us joy, peace, and contentment. Those are the blessings I want for you today!

Special Notes:

The Mind of Christ

…But we have the mind of Christ.

I CORINTHIANS 2:16

Today's Life Brightener

God has given us his Spirit, who gives us power, wisdom, and guidance. I pray that you'll sense the Holy Spirit's presence in your life today.

Special Notes:

The New You

You were taught…to put on the new self,
created to be like God….
EPHESIANS 4:22,24

Today's Life Brightener

Christ gives us a new way of thinking, changing each of us into a new person. It makes me happy when I see God's work in your life!

Special Notes:

Two-Part Harmony

…live in harmony with one another….

1 PETER 3:8

Today's Life Brightener

Sometimes we have disagreements, but we never stop loving each other. Your commitment to me brings harmony to my life.

Special Notes:

CARING

Deeper Love

Above all, love each other deeply….

1 PETER 4:8

Today's Life Brightener

When we're not getting along, it's never because we've stopped loving each other. Our love endures because it comes from God. Thanks for loving me so deeply!

Special Notes:

Thanks for Caring

…it was good of you to share in my troubles.

PHILIPPIANS 4:14

Today's Life Brightener

You always come to my rescue just when I need it. You understand my needs like no one else. What would I do without you?

Special Notes:

A Wonderful Gift

A wife of noble character who can find?
She is worth far more than rubies.

PROVERBS 31:10

Today's Life Brightener

My life changed forever the day I met you. You're a wonderful gift from God, and you mean more to me than I can ever express!

Special Notes:

● -- ●

● -- ●

● -- ●

● -- ●

Inner Beauty

…the unfading beauty of a gentle and quiet spirit…

is of great worth in God's sight.

1 PETER 3:4

Today's Life Brightener

You are beautiful beyond measure. Your gentle and quiet spirit calms me and gives me confidence. You're such a blessing to me!

Special Notes:

Don't Worry!

So don't be afraid; you are worth more than many sparrows.

MATTHEW 10:31

Today's Life Brightener

A lot of things cause worry, but God promises to take care of us. You're valuable to God, and you're also valuable to me. I love you!

Special Notes:

Real Commitment

…a married woman is bound to her husband

as long as he is alive….

ROMANS 7:2

Today's Life Brightener

When we stood before God on our wedding day, I vowed that only death would separate us. I meant it then, and I mean it even more today. I'm in our marriage for life!

Special Notes:

Hearts Joined Together

…she shall be called "woman,"
for she was taken out of man.

GENESIS 2:23

Today's Life Brightener

God has knitted us together in a lifetime bond, and my commitment to you runs deeper every day. God did some of his best work when he gave you to me!

Special Notes:

A Loving Promise

When a man makes a vow to the LORD…
he must not break his word….

NUMBERS 30:2

Today's Life Brightener

I gladly vowed before God to love, honor, and cherish you. I love making good on this promise, so tell me what I can do for you today.

Special Notes:

●--●

●--●

●--●

●--●

A Great Listener

Everyone should be quick to listen, slow to speak….

JAMES 1:19

Today's Life Brightener

God gave me two ears but only one mouth, so I want to talk less and listen more. Tonight, you talk and I'll listen!

Special Notes:

Hearing Your Heart

He who answers before listening—
that is his folly and his shame.
PROVERBS 18:13

Today's Life Brightener

I want to hear your heart, so I'm committed to listening more carefully. No assumptions here—I want to understand you more.

Special Notes:

Graceful Speech

Let your conversation be always full of grace, seasoned with salt,

so that you may know how to answer everyone.

COLOSSIANS 4:6

Today's Life Brightener

I want my words to nourish your soul with grace. Today, know that you're the best thing in my life!

Special Notes:

The Path of Contentment

But godliness with contentment is great gain.

I TIMOTHY 6:6

Today's Life Brightener

God blesses us when we put him first. I find my greatest contentment when we're following Christ together.

Special Notes:

Trusting the Provider

But if we have food and clothing, we will be content with that.

I TIMOTHY 6:8

Today's Life Brightener

God isn't concerned about our bank account; he cares about *us*. Let's trust him to provide everything we need.

Special Notes:

A Better Focus

But seek first his kingdom and his righteousness,
and all these things will be given to you as well.

MATTHEW 6:33

Today's Life Brightener

When God has first place in our hearts, he gives us everything we need today.
God knows our needs better than we do, so let's rest in his promise.

Special Notes:

Sharing Burdens

Carry each other's burdens….

GALATIANS 6:2

Today's Life Brightener

Life's challenges are too heavy for just one person, so let me help carry your burdens. I'm ready, so just give me the word!

Special Notes:

A True Partner

Be…patient, bearing with one another in love.

EPHESIANS 4:2

Today's Life Brightener

Sometimes I'm guilty of doing things without thinking. I want to slow down and be a true partner to you. What burden can I bear for you today?

Special Notes:

My Top Concern

But a married man is concerned about the affairs of this world—

how he can please his wife.

1 CORINTHIANS 7:33

Today's Life Brightener

I want to please you in a way that's pleasing to the Lord. So depend on me! You're my *top* concern.

Special Notes:

Real Hope

Why are you downcast, O my soul?
Why so disturbed within me?
Put your hope in God….

PSALM 42:5

Today's Life Brightener

You've been dealing with some tough stuff lately. But remember that you're always on God's mind, and he gives us real hope. I'm praying for you today.

Special Notes:

God's Help

…My soul is downcast within me;

therefore I will remember you….

PSALM 42:6

Today's Life Brightener

Don't let life steal your peace. You're not alone in this struggle. God is here to help you, and so am I. Let's face this together.

Special Notes:

Strength in Hope

...And we rejoice in the hope of the glory of God....
And hope does not disappoint us....

ROMANS 5:2,5

Today's Life Brightener

Life sometimes disappoints us, but God never does. He is eager to bless us with joy and hope. Let's trust God to see us through!

Special Notes:

FAILURE

A Merciful Spirit

…Mercy triumphs over judgment!

JAMES 2:13

Today's Life Brightener

Sometimes I fail you even when I'm trying hard not to. And when I mess up, your merciful spirit triumphs. That's special to me.

Special Notes:

God's Mercy

...In his great mercy he has given us new birth into a living hope
through the resurrection of Jesus Christ from the dead.

1 PETER 1:3

Today's Life Brightener

God's hope is alive and available right now. I know I sometimes fail you and God both. I'm thankful for his mercy, so let's enjoy the hope he brings.

Special Notes:

Saved by Mercy

[H]e saved us, not because of righteous things
we had done, but because of his mercy....

TITUS 3:5

Today's Life Brightener

God never sees our failures as a reason to reject us; rather he offers mercy to save us. Our failures are his opportunities to open doors of hope for us.

Special Notes:

Jesus Is Your Helper

...The Lord is my helper....

HEBREWS 13:6

Today's Life Brightener

While you're on this business trip, rushing to meetings and making presentations, I'm praying that you will sense God's help. And I can't wait for you to get home!

Special Notes:

Faith, Not Fear

In God, whose word I praise,
in God I trust; I will not be afraid....

PSALM 56:4

Today's Life Brightener

No matter what you face today, God is on your side. So look up when you're feeling down. God will overcome the opposition!

Special Notes:

God Goes with You

For the LORD your God is the one who goes with you
to fight for you…to give you victory.

DEUTERONOMY 20:4

Today's Life Brightener

Whatever is worrying you today, remember that it's not your battle; it's God's.
He promises to fight for you. With God, you're always on the winning side!

Special Notes:

Freedom in Forgiveness

Praise the LORD…
who forgives all your sins
and heals all your diseases.

PSALM 103:2-3

Today's Life Brightener

God doesn't forgive *some* of our sins. He forgives them *all*. We can enjoy his freedom because we're forgiven completely. God is so good!

Special Notes:

Hidden Faults

…Forgive my hidden faults.

PSALM 19:12

Today's Life Brightener

Sometimes I hurt you without realizing it. I want to confess this to God, and to you. Please forgive me.

Special Notes:

Grace at Work

...God made you alive with Christ. He forgave us all our sins.

COLOSSIANS 2:13

Today's Life Brightener

God forgives our sins, but I continue to stumble. I'm thankful that in your love you help me see where I need to grow. God's grace is at work through you!

Special Notes:

Clarity, Not Confusion

...he will make your paths straight.

PROVERBS 3:6

Today's Life Brightener

Life can get frustrating at times, so I'm glad God is guiding us. I love following him together!

Special Notes:

God's Path

I know, O LORD, that a man's life is not his own;

it is not for man to direct his steps.

JEREMIAH 10:23

Today's Life Brightener

We both want the best for our marriage, so let's allow God to direct our steps. He will show us the path he wants us to take.

Special Notes:

Directed by God

A man's steps are directed by the LORD....

PROVERBS 20:24

Today's Life Brightener

It's comforting to know that God directs our ways, especially when the destination is unclear. Thanks for encouraging me to trust God's guidance.

Special Notes:

Love Without Limits

...you know God—or rather are known by God....

GALATIANS 4:9

Today's Life Brightener

God knows you like no one else, and he loves you without limits. Rest in his love, because he knows *everything* about us, and he still loves us!

Special Notes:

Unfailing Compassion

Because of the LORD's great love we are not consumed,
for his compassions never fail.

LAMENTATIONS 3:22

Today's Life Brightener

There is never a moment when God is not watching over you. Throughout the day, Jesus surrounds you with his mercy. You are precious to God!

Special Notes:

Always Faithful

God, who has called you into fellowship with his Son
Jesus Christ our Lord, is faithful.

1 CORINTHIANS 1:9

Today's Life Brightener

God has never failed us in the past, and he won't refuse to help us now. Let's commit our concerns to him and see what he'll do.

Special Notes:

Plans for Success

"For I know the plans I have for you," declares the LORD,
"plans to prosper you and not to harm you,
plans to give you hope and a future."

JEREMIAH 29:11

Today's Life Brightener

God knows what's best for us, even when we don't understand all that's going on in our lives. Let's join God on this adventure and see where his plans lead us!

Special Notes:

Perfect Plans

Many are the plans in a man's heart,
but it is the LORD's purpose that prevails.

PROVERBS 19:21

Today's Life Brightener

It's good to plan for the future, but let's make plans with the understanding that God is still in charge. His plans for us are perfect!

Special Notes:

Tomorrow's Joy

There is surely a future hope for you,
and your hope will not be cut off.

PROVERBS 23:18

Today's Life Brightener

God has a wonderful hope waiting for you down the road. While today might
be tough, trust the Lord to bring you joy tomorrow.

Special Notes:

Our Rich Provider

Command those who are rich in this present world…to put their hope in God, who richly provides us with everything for our enjoyment.

I TIMOTHY 6:17

Today's Life Brightener

No one is wealthier than God, so he will never run out of anything we need. In fact, he already provided so much of what I need when he brought us together!

Special Notes:

●--●

●--●

●--●

●--●

The Best Things

...no good thing does he withhold
from those whose walk is blameless.
PSALM 84:11

Today's Life Brightener

As we lovingly follow the Lord together, we will receive his goodness in abundance. Nothing will be withheld—absolutely nothing!

Special Notes:

Just What Is Needed

Abraham answered, "God himself will provide the lamb
for the burnt offering, my son."...

GENESIS 22:8

Today's Life Brightener

Remember, Abraham trusted God even when it didn't make sense, and God provided in a miraculous way. Let's count on God to provide exactly what we need today!

Special Notes:

•--•

•--•

•--•

•--•

Thank You!

Whatever you do, work at it with all your heart,
as working for the Lord....

COLOSSIANS 3:23

Today's Life Brightener

I know you're under pressure at work. I want you to know how much I appreciate and respect the way you provide for our family!

Special Notes:

I Respect You

However, each one of you also must love his wife as he loves himself,
and the wife must respect her husband.

EPHESIANS 5:33

Today's Life Brightener

Honoring and respecting you makes me happy. I can't thank God enough for bringing you into my life.

Special Notes:

I'm Here, Always

Be devoted to one another in brotherly love.
Honor one another above yourselves.

ROMANS 12:10

Today's Life Brightener

Please don't ever doubt my devoted love for you. No other person will ever stand between us. I thought you'd like to hear that today!

Special Notes:

I Prefer You

For this reason a man will leave his father and mother….

GENESIS 2:24

Today's Life Brightener

As much as we love our parents, it's the Lord and us now. I'm glad we're on our own together!

Special Notes:

No Longer Two

...the two will become one flesh.

MATTHEW 19:5

Today's Life Brightener

Our bond is so secure that only God can separate us at the end of our lives. I love being like-minded and single-hearted with you!

Special Notes:

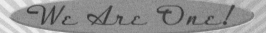

For this reason a man will…be united to his wife.

MARK 10:7

Today's Life Brightener

We're joined for life. It's a good thing that God made us one, since I'd never want to live my life any other way!

Special Notes:

Complete Devotion

Love the LORD your God with all your heart and with all your soul
and with all your strength.

DEUTERONOMY 6:5

Today's Life Brightener

When we love God with our entire being, we'll see good things spill over into
our marriage. Let's help each other love God.

Special Notes:

Finding Stability

…just as you received Christ Jesus as Lord, continue to live in him,

rooted and built up in him….

COLOSSIANS 2:6-7

Today's Life Brightener

Change is never easy. It threatens to throw our life off course. I'm glad we're rooted in Jesus, because he *never* changes!

Special Notes:

Christ in Us

For to me, to live is Christ....

PHILIPPIANS 1:21

Today's Life Brightener

We belong to each other, and I wouldn't want it any other way. But God has a higher claim on our lives. I'm thankful that he is in charge!

Special Notes:

Financial Worries

No one can serve two masters. Either he will hate the one and love the other, or he will be devoted to the one and despise the other. You cannot serve both God and Money.

MATTHEW 6:24

Today's Life Brightener

There never seems to be enough money to cover everything. But God is our security, so let's commit our concerns to him. He'll take care of us.

Special Notes:

Every Good Thing

...whoever loves wealth is never satisfied with his income....

ECCLESIASTES 5:10

Today's Life Brightener

God is the only One who can satisfy us, and he gives us every good thing. Let's help each other trust him with our financial needs.

Special Notes:

Generosity

Give, and it will be given to you....

LUKE 6:38

Today's Life Brightener

God promises that whatever we give to him and to others will come back as a blessing to us. Let's see where the adventure of giving takes us!

Special Notes:

PATIENCE

The Path of Patience

But the fruit of the Spirit is…patience….

GALATIANS 5:22

Today's Life Brightener

The world resembles a rat race, and it's tempting to expect quick results. But God has his own purposes, so let's wait and trust his timetable.

Special Notes:

God's Timing

But when the time had fully come, God sent his Son….

GALATIANS 4:4

Today's Life Brightener

God's work follows his perfect timing, and he is never late. The Lord knows what's best for us today. He hasn't forgotten what we need.

Special Notes:

Patient Love

And we urge you,…be patient with everyone.

I THESSALONIANS 5:14

Today's Life Brightener

God is always patient with us, and he directs us to be patient with others. Thanks for loving me with the patience that God gives.

Special Notes:

What Do You Need?

Do not deprive each other except by mutual consent and for a time,

so that you may devote yourselves to prayer....

I CORINTHIANS 7:5

Today's Life Brightener

I want to give you what you need. Take my heart, my affection, and my body.
Tell me what you want from me today!

Special Notes:

●--●

●--●

●--●

●--●

PHYSICAL RELATIONSHIP

I Belong to You

The wife's body does not belong to her alone but also to her husband.
In the same way, the husband's body does not belong to him alone
but also to his wife.

1 CORINTHIANS 7:4

Today's Life Brightener

I belong to you and only to you, and it's my joy to satisfy your deepest needs. I
can't wait for us to be together!

Special Notes:

We Fit!

The man said,
"This is now bone of my bones
and flesh of my flesh…."

GENESIS 2:23

Today's Life Brightener

We were created to fit together in a one-flesh relationship. I love finding ways to make our bond even stronger!

Special Notes:

PRIORITIES

The Best Decision

...First seek the counsel of the LORD.

1 KINGS 22:5

Today's Life Brightener

It's never easy to decide between two good things. If you're facing a big decision at work, or even a small one, ask God about it. He's always right!

Special Notes:

First Love

You have persevered and have endured hardships for my name....
Yet I hold this against you: You have forsaken your first love.

REVELATION 2:3-4

Today's Life Brightener

We'll never leave each other, but God is our first love. As we cherish each other, let's remember God's claim on us. He deserves to come first!

Special Notes:

The Life of Service

...they gave themselves first to the Lord and then to us
in keeping with God's will.

2 CORINTHIANS 8:5

Today's Life Brightener

With so many people needing your attention, it's no wonder you get worn out.
But remember this: God is first and others are second.

Special Notes:

●---●

●---●

●---●

●---●

Removing Obstacles

…let us throw off everything that hinders
and the sin that so easily entangles….
HEBREWS 12:1

Today's Life Brightener

If we allow anything to come between God and us, we'll soon notice a distance between the two of us. Let's ask God to reveal anything that displeases him.

Special Notes:

Turning Toward God

[I]f my people…will humble themselves and pray and seek my face
and turn from their wicked ways,
then will I hear from heaven and will forgive their sin….

2 CHRONICLES 7:14

Today's Life Brightener

Repentance is rejecting sin in favor of obeying our loving God. Let's ask him to show us anything that might be holding us back.

Special Notes:

●---●

●---●

●---●

●---●

God Comes First

Dear children, keep yourselves from idols.

1 JOHN 5:21

Today's Life Brightener

It's easy to put other things ahead of God. Let's ask God to open our eyes to the things that compete for our devotion.

Special Notes:

Priceless Riches

...since you are a son, God has made you also an heir.

GALATIANS 4:7

Today's Life Brightener

Jesus has given us priceless riches to enjoy—treasures too great to be measured. And of all the visible treasures in my life, you're the greatest!

Special Notes:

Incredible Wealth

For in him you have been enriched in every way....

1 CORINTHIANS 1:5

Today's Life Brightener

In Christ we have unsurpassed riches, so the wealthiest person on earth is the one who follows Christ. Let's enjoy and use the riches God has given us.

Special Notes:

Crowned with Glory

When I consider your heavens,…what is man that you are
mindful of him…? You made him a little lower than the heavenly beings
and crowned him with glory and honor.

PSALM 8:3-5

Today's Life Brightener

God has adorned you with glory and honor, making you something very
special. Your stock is high in God's sight—and in mine!

Special Notes:

•--•

•--•

•--•

•--•

Guarding Against Sin

But we prayed to our God and posted a guard
day and night to meet this threat.

NEHEMIAH 4:9

Today's Life Brightener

Temptations are enemies that can attack at any time. Let's pray and post a guard
to protect our relationship from enemies.

Special Notes:

●-------------------------------------●

●-------------------------------------●

●-------------------------------------●

●-------------------------------------●

The Best Passion

I made a covenant with my eyes
not to look lustfully at a girl.

JOB 31:1

Today's Life Brightener

We're constantly bombarded with images designed to distract us from each other, but *you* are my passion. I just wanted you to know that.

Special Notes:

God's Power

Watch and pray so that you will not fall into temptation.
The spirit is willing, but the body is weak.

MARK 14:38

Today's Life Brightener

We can't depend on our own strength. We need God's power to resist temptation. I'm praying that you'll experience his power today!

Special Notes:

Time to Rest

There is a time for everything,
and a season for every activity under heaven.

ECCLESIASTES 3:1

Today's Life Brightener

You work really hard, and I appreciate it. But life is more than work. How can I free you up so you can rest and find refreshment?

Special Notes:

●--●

●--●

●--●

●--●

Serving God

The night is nearly over; the day is almost here....

ROMANS 13:12

Today's Life Brightener

It won't be long until Jesus comes again, so let's find ways to invest in God's kingdom. I love it when we serve God together!

Special Notes:

- -

- -

- -

- -

Maximum Living

Be very careful, then, how you live…
making the most of every opportunity….

EPHESIANS 5:15-16

Today's Life Brightener

We are free to decide how to use our time. Let's make God—and each other—
our top priorities this week. I want to invest in us!

Special Notes:

Finding Strength

...For when I am weak, then I am strong.

2 CORINTHIANS 12:10

Today's Life Brightener

When we face difficulties, Christ has a chance to show his power through us. I'm asking him to pour his strength through you today!

Special Notes:

●--●

●--●

●--●

●--●

God's Power

...God chose the weak things of the world to shame the strong.

1 CORINTHIANS 1:27

Today's Life Brightener

Many heroes in the Bible were weak, and still they won amazing battles. When you think about it, our weakness doesn't matter, because our God is *strong!*

Special Notes:

●--●

●--●

●--●

●--●

The Perfect Refuge

The eternal God is your refuge,
and underneath are the everlasting arms....

DEUTERONOMY 33:27

Today's Life Brightener

God won't let you fall; his everlasting arms will sustain you. So lean back and rest in the safety of his protection. God is for you!

Special Notes:

Keeping It Short

If anyone considers himself religious
and yet does not keep a tight rein on his tongue,
he deceives himself….

JAMES 1:26

Today's Life Brightener

Sometimes I talk too much and say things I shouldn't, so let me keep this short:
I love you, today and always!

Special Notes:

Words of Blessing

Do not let any unwholesome talk come out of your mouths,
but only what is helpful for building others up….

EPHESIANS 4:29

Today's Life Brightener

I want to bless you with my words, to express my love and to build you up.
Consider this note a message from my heart to yours. I love you!

Special Notes:

Pleasing Talk

May the words of my mouth and the meditation of my heart

be pleasing in your sight, O LORD....

PSALM 19:14

Today's Life Brightener

I want the Lord to be pleased with what I say to you and about you. I love to brag about you, and I love talking with you. Tonight let's get alone just to talk!

Special Notes:

●--●

●--●

●--●

●--●